Drug Slaves

Drug Slaves

Ibrahim Muhammed Bashir

authorHOUSE®

AuthorHouse™ UK Ltd.
1663 Liberty Drive
Bloomington, IN 47403 USA
www.authorhouse.co.uk
Phone: 0800.197.4150

Published by AuthorHouse   07/01/2013

ISBN: 978-1-4817-8393-4 (sc)
ISBN: 978-1-4817-8392-7 (e)

Contents

Part I

Part II

To all the drug addicts who went through counselling and rehabilitation and were fully integrated into society.

Acknowledgements

I thank God for making this book see the light of day. My appreciation goes to everyone who had made contributions at one stage or the other, while I put this book together.

To those clients who volunteered their true life stories, I say thank you.

My gratitude also goes to my family for their ongoing understanding and support.

Foreword

The effort of the author Ibrahim Muhammed Bashir is highly appreciated. Appreciated in a sense that the writing style is such that both the Drug Slave and their friends are able to realize their power of choice even in a warm loving family environment.

The title of the book "Drug Slaves" is very appropriate since it is by choice and not by conviction that some youths have chosen to be enslaved in an atmosphere when they could have chosen freedom. While Vincent decided on a Role model of the smoker, other youth chose Role models that were more decent. Vincent's opportunity to be kicked out of the University could not have been truncated if he chose Role models with decent values. The Author also depicted the influence of parental guidance in this look. Parents are therefore urged to provide decent Role models to their children.

Bashir,

The author more or less exposed the reader to the negative influences of commercials such as the man depicted as 'Mr. Cool' with his cigarettes and alcohol. It should be emphasized that those who sell cigarettes and alcohol are doing so to make money and they can spend any amount to promote their sales, irrespective of how much damage is inflicted on those who choose to be convinced by their adverts.

The author more or less concluded this book with the introduction of the National Drug Law Enforcement Agency (N.D.L.E.A) rehabilitation center as an appropriate place for many youth who are already enslaved to Drugs and Alcohol. This is also an ideal opportunity for parents who are also struggling to correct their children's drug and alcohol bad habits.

The book is strongly recommended to Parents, Teachers, Counselors, Psychologists and Religious leaders who are trying to assist children and youth who are already Drug Slaves.

Professor Akin Odebunmi

Part I

Chapter One

Vincent's Role Model

A handsome man, smartly dressed in a suit, tie, and shining black shoes, was shown on the popular television station called Eagle Television Authority (ETA). He walked with a clouded look on his face for a while but smiled with relief on seeing a man standing at the roadside who handed him a cigarette. The man lit the cigarette; he inhaled and then coughed up a lungful of smoke and smiled. 'This makes me feel good!' he said, spreading his hands apart.

Vincent watched as the shot zoomed in; the man's face was turned to the sky, his eyes were closed, and he was smiling. The on-screen image shrank and then disappeared. Immediately, bold writing appeared, saying, 'Smokers are liable to die young!' Vincent did not grasp exactly what the words meant.

'Son, I thought you had gone to bed.' Vincent recognized his father's dry voice. He smiled without looking at Mr Udomu. 'Daddy, you know my role model is the cigarette advert on the television, which I watch before bed every day,' he said.

'So now that the advert is over, why can't you go to bed?'

'Yes, Daddy.' He walked to the mattress at the corner of his room. 'Goodnight!' he said.

Mr Udomu's house was a four-bedroom flat. The sitting room contained an up-to-date entertainment set. Modern and traditional African art hung on the walls, and lively photographs of Mr Udomu, his wife, Vincent, and Nnamdi were everywhere. Vincent's room was Spartan; there were only a few pieces of furniture scattered around, including a huge mattress on the floor and a mini fridge in a corner.

Vincent walked out of the flat, banging the door in the process. He watched the flowers being blown by the wind as he stood still at the corridor. 'Are you all right?' Nnamdi asked from behind him.

'Yeah, I'm just thinking about a captivating little advert that leads to temptation. I admire the young man's taste and smart outfit.' Vincent said.

'You mean the cigarette man, as always?'

'Yeah, I guess I've had enough of that man's design, and I wondered at the brain behind the scene.'

Nnamdi moved nearer. 'Don't be deceived by his outfit! It would be better if you got in and did something nice before dusk and kept your mouth shut about that,' he added.

Vincent was always bored with Nnamdi's ways of doing things. *I've heard his words before, and they don't really amount to anything,* he thought.

The sun was still very hot and strong, and there was only a mild breeze coming from the eastern part of the compound. There was no sign of a rain cloud anywhere.

Vincent glanced down at his father, who was facing away from him on the corner of a seat. From that angle; Vincent could see his father light a cigarette. 'What's do you think of the weather, Dad?' Vincent asked, walking towards him.

'Very boring, my son!'

'Could that be the reason you are smoking a cigarette?' Vincent asked, almost in his father's ear.

'Yeah, but cigarettes are not for boys your age,' Mr Udomu said.

'Vincent,' Stella interrupted, walking toward their position. 'Get in here this minute and help your brother with the cleaning. Then she looked at her husband. 'I thought we agreed that you would smoke only when the boys are away.'

'You always ruin everything without any reason!' he answered harshly. Stella stood and stared at him for a while.

'It's cool to smoke a cigarette on this hot afternoon, but I don't want my kids to get addicted so fast,' she said. Her voice was cold and grating.

Mr Udomu gently got to his feet and walked towards the flowers without speaking. 'You can just wander around and do what you like. After all, it's the weekend; enjoy your packets of cigarettes, but not when my kids are with you,' she added and made her way to the backyard.

A tap sounded on the door and Stella came in, carrying a bundle of wet clothes she had washed and then dried on the rope in the backyard earlier. She looked at Vincent and then at Nnamdi, who were both sitting on a couch in the sitting room.

Vincent expected her to say something but saw her walk towards her room without looking back. She went into her room and shut the door. 'I'm sure you feel uncomfortable seeing Mummy.' Nnamdi broke the silence. There was a malicious look in his eyes. Vincent ran his fingers through his itchy hair. 'I don't like how you're looking at me! You all suspect that I took a cigarette, but what is bad about it? Daddy and the man on Eagle Television Authority smoke and both are fine and happy—'

'Yeah, that's where the trouble is going to start for you. You are just nine years old, and you say and believe that every ugly thing people do is good,' Nnamdi interrupted.

'Let me inform Dad of what you just said, and you will wish it had turned out differently,' Vincent said.

Nnamdi walked to his room, slamming the door in the process. He moved over to the window. Vincent should be careful choosing his words, he thought, staring at a deserted street and then the sun that was gradually falling below the horizon. Vincent walked over to his room and lay very still on the bed, vaguely conscious that he ought to be doing something very important, but what it was, he couldn't remember.

He moved his long legs, feeling the smooth linen sliding over his skin. What did he have to do? He couldn't remember. He heard a knock at the gate outside. His heart skipped a beat, but still he didn't move. Now he remembered. *Sule's invitation, of course,* he thought, and moved slightly less rhythmically towards the gate.

Vincent pulled open the small gate and saw a tall, very clean-looking Sule in white clothes. 'Sule,' he called.

'I just came,' Sule replied.

'You couldn't knock at the gate?'

'I was about to do that when I heard a tapping sound at the door and paused, waiting for the door to be opened,' Sule explained.

'You are good to look at today.' Vincent complimented his friend and saw the cynical look in his eyes as they walked towards a big rock close to a deserted path overlooking the waterfront.

'Sit here!' Sule ordered.

'What are we going to do here?' Vincent asked.

'Just watch!' Sule confidently lit a cigarette.

'You smoke?'

'Oh yes. My father and his driver do. For that reason, I found it difficult to resist,' Sule said hoarsely.

'Does your father know you smoke cigarettes?'

'No! He warned me not to try it, saying that only older men smoke. I know it will be a grave misfortune for me the day I'm caught,' he added.

Vincent drew a deep breath. 'I'm surprised you are ignoring your father's instructions.' As he said this, two boys of about their same age walked up.

Vincent shook his head and told the group, 'My father taught me that one can inhale as many cigarettes as he or she wants when one is older.' The boys looked at each other and gave a squeal of laughter. 'You're not as nice of a little boy as you look. You will soon be your father's shadow like we are ours.' Sule said, shifting a little nearer.

Vincent was so confused. 'I always had a fear of things I couldn't understand. I got a hell of a shock whenever my mother accused me of smoking, and I think you boys are dangerous.'

'Wow!' said a short boy in a blue coat and a peaked cap. He took off his hat. 'That shouldn't bother you, pal; Sule always says that you like the advert on ETA, and the day you lose the opportunity to watch it, you will feel like someone who lost an elephant. Isn't that man like us? Or is it not the same type of cigarette? So, get rid of the pretence and join us, if you so desire.'

Vincent gave the boy a quick glance. 'I don't fancy harsh words, and I think you are using them,' he said with intensity.

'Let's not have any trouble; I may look little, but I'm tougher than you think. Beat it and get that thin, wolfish face of yours away from here,' the boy said, waving his arms violently.

'I want to smoke but not with your type of cigarettes.' Vincent said and started walking towards the waterfall.

The boy felt extraordinarily unimportant and wished he had never spoken with Vincent. 'Sule,' he called. 'You suggested that this naughty boy may like a taste of cigarette. Tell him that I will knock him down if he talks to me in that tone again,' the boy said, tapping the ash of his cigarette and stepping towards Vincent.

'I'm only giving you grace because of my friend.' Vincent harshly shifted his eyes. Sule looked through him. Vincent did not give in to the pleasure of embarrassing the boy. He silently watched the two boys climbing down the rock rather gingerly, and then he turned Sule's way. 'Don't dream of inviting me here next time,' he warned Sule and walked away.

Chapter Two

A Taste of Cigarettes

———○ ○———

Years passed like a day. Vincent was now in Senior Secondary Class I; he felt serene and relaxed. Vincent sat quietly, watching the students waiting for the bell to ring. 'Hello!' he saw a boy smiling at him. The boy had glistening white teeth and sparkling eyes.

'I'm Ojo; can you please accompany me to my house? It is just a kilometre away from the school.'

'Aren't you the new boy that started class last week?' Vincent asked with a pleasant voice.

'Yes, I am. I attended Sky Unlimited Secondary School for my junior classes, but my father prefers Global Future for reasons known only to him,' Ojo said. The two boys laughed. 'I'd like us to be friends,' he added.

Vincent smiled. 'That sounds good. Come on; let's go before the break's over.'

They walked to a tall building that looked like a private dwelling. 'This is my house,' Ojo said, and they ascended the crescent-shaped steps to the front door. Ojo opened the door and they walked in. 'Mummy may have left for the market.' He started talking about how his mum bought a lot of books from the market and gave him money, which he had used to buy cigarettes the previous day.

'Suppose you get me some breakfast and stop chatting,' Vincent said. 'Get me bread. I'm hungry.'

Ojo made a little face. 'There is no bread.'

'Coffee . . . ?'

'Yes, but no bread until my mum returns. Ojo answered and walked to the kitchen. He soon returned and handed Vincent a cup of coffee. He pulled a stool up, sat down, and crossed his legs. Vincent took two quick sips of the coffee and said that they should leave before the school break was over. 'Yes, let me pick up my textbook,' Ojo said. He soon returned with the book from his room, and they made their way to school.

Students were outside, buying food from vendors, chatting, and walking around. 'You see! The break is still going on; come on, let's go to the back of the school, under the orange tree. I'd like to enjoy my usual stuff,' Ojo said.

'No, you go; I'll wait in the school library until you come,' Vincent replied.

'Please come with me. I will not stay for long,' Ojo pleaded, and they both walked to back of the school building.

Ojo sat on a small rock under the tree. Vincent sat down near him. Ojo felt in his pocket for his cigarette case. Vincent watched him sternly as he lit a cigarette.

'Do you care for a smoke?' Ojo asked.

'Why do you smoke?' Vincent asked seriously. He recalled the advert man saying, 'This makes me feel good.'

'Come on, taste it, and you will like it a lot,' Ojo said and filled his lungs with the cigarette smoke. Vincent watched him inhale.

It may be an interesting tasting one, he thought and leaned his head back against the tree.

'I'm enjoying myself enormously; I wish you would have a taste.'

I can lay the foundation; after all, Father has one whenever he is bored, Vincent thought. 'Let me have one!' he said.

'Now, that sounds exciting,' Ojo said, handing him a cigarette. Vincent collected the cigarette and lend forward as he used Ojo's lighter. He felt serene and happy. He relaxed for a while and stood on his feet when he heard the bell ring.

'Hello!' said Vincent.

'Why, hello. Aren't you late?' the security man said in response.

'I'm sorry, sir.'

'That's what you boys always say; perhaps you want a reputation for arriving late?'

'No, sir.' After a moment's delay, the short, dapper man opened the gate.

'Thank you, sir,' said both boys, and they ran to their class.

Two days later, Vincent sat on a plastic chair in the backyard of the flat, smoking cigarettes. *My first experience of seeing a smoker in the ETA advert gave me a little satisfaction, and I rather wanted to experiment myself. I had years of wondering what the man felt, as the cigarette helped him through depression. Now that I know what it feels like, it is pretty good. Yes, it makes one feel the good side of life!* he thought.

'Vincent.' Stella, Vincent's mum—walked up to him. 'What on earth are you doing with a cigarette?'

'Smoking, Mummy,' he answered, looking at the cigarette.

'What . . . ? Let me have that now.' She took the cigarette from him. 'You ought to be awfully sorry for this.'

Vincent got slowly on his feet and walked past his mother. 'You've spoilt my day, Mummy. Isn't that more important than me being sorry?' She looked down at him thoughtfully. He added, 'You know you deprived me for several years, but you can't now that I know what it tastes like.' Vincent climbed the steps; he opened the door and looked the mum up and down.

'They say that when a boy gets tough, use a rod to make him change before he gets himself into big trouble. Maybe that is what you need, Vincent,' she said and walked into the flat.

'You have said nothing about Vincent's stubborn acts,' Stella said to her husband.

Mr Udomu got up slowly and walked over to the window. 'He will change. All he needs is time,' he answered, rolling down the window to spit into the dark.

The next day during one of the school breaks, Ojo and Vincent walked past an unfinished building. Vincent became conscious of a considerable amount of noise and laughter drifting through the large, open windows. It seemed that boys and noise were inevitably linked together. 'Come on,' he said.

They walked into the large building through open double doors. A number of students were standing around with wrapped marijuana in their hands. They all looked in Ojo and Vincent's direction; a girl moved towards them.

'I don't remember ever seeing a photograph of either of you. Meeting you here for the first time comes as a shock! Anyway, you can join us, but you must not let the school authorities know about this.' Ojo and Vincent nodded, and they walked over to where the small group was standing.

'Hi guys!'

Next, George walked in. 'Vincent!' he shouted.

'George.' They embraced each other.

'I didn't expect to see a bad boy here.'

'So this is where you always leave class to go! Today I have caught you,' Vincent said, jovially.

'Let them taste some of this good-quality stuff,' George ordered, smiling.

A girl, Saratu, handed Vincent and Ojo wrapped marijuana. She was above the average height, small-featured, and perfectly groomed in her neat uniform, but her expression took away everything that could have counted in her favour. With her flawed make-up application, she looked like a very expensive streetwalker. Her eyes were cold, calculating, and vicious.

Vincent smoked for a while and smiled because he felt good. 'I would like to be a member,' Vincent said, wandering over to the window. George could see that Vincent was still high, but his face was very serious.

'Simply contribute a small amount for the stuff, and you are a member!' Suddenly they heard movement outside, and for several seconds they stood still and were so silent they only made little sputtering noises.

'We would be glad to have you both. As you can see, we are very few,' George said, patting Vincent's on the back. 'I'd like to see a lot more of you,' he added and made his way towards the school. The boys followed his example, one after another, and then the two girls and Vincent and Ojo last.

The school grounds were very quiet, and all the students were gone. 'Where will I tell my dad I went after school?' Vincent cried, looking at the locked school gate.

'You amuse me, Vincent. You should be patient. Your father will have no option but to come back looking for you, and when he does, tell him you are sorry that you went for football training.' Ojo advised.

'You are right!'

'Why don't you start walking home?' Ojo asked.

'No, I'm scared. I might run into him, and he may question me or think that I'm not coming from the football field,' Vincent answered steadily.

They were silent for a while. Ojo looked at him at last and said, 'It's damn strange how things happen, isn't it? Maybe when you get out of this and look back on it, you'll be able to see why it had to happen.'

Vincent squinted, as if to see his friend more clearly. 'You think so?' he asked, frowning.

'Yeah, especially considering that you were interested in being a regular member in a group with those who are never conscious of time'

'I must speak to George about it tomorrow,' Vincent said. This sudden outburst shook Ojo, as he knew how foul George and his group were.

There was heavy breeze, and Vincent looked up. The sky was full of dark clouds. 'Wow! It is unbelievable that my dad will relax without checking on me again.'

'It's not his fault; moreover, you don't know how worried they are right now.' Vincent looked at Ojo, feeling that his friend was too sincere for his liking. 'Listen, I would like to go home. It will soon begin to rain. Won't you come with me?'

'No, I will be fine.

Ojo walked fast, leaving Vincent standing very straight, with his eyes flashing, his hands clenched by his side and his school bag on the floor beside him. Mr Udomu drove up and came to a halt in front of the school. He walked past Vincent without taking notice of him and continued walking. Mr Udomu rapped on the small gate of the school and threw it open. 'Vincent!' he shouted. He looked upset.

Vincent suddenly picked up his bag and walked toward the school gate in the heavy breeze. 'Daddy!' he called and ran to his father. Mr Udomu angrily held his hand, took him to the car, and drove off.

Chapter Three

Cough Syrup

———⊖ ⊖———

Vincent got out of the car and staggered into the flat through the heavy rain. He sat down on a wooden stool in his room and wrapped his arms around himself. 'Where are you coming from? You spoilt child!' the mum said as she walked in.

'Woman, can't you see that the boy is cold? I expected you to help him with his clothes instead of shouting; we are lucky we found him,' Mr Udomu said.

"Well', I've got no time to assist.' She left the room.

'Don't repeat this behaviour, Son,' Mr Udomu said and shut the door behind him.

The next day as Nnamdi sat watching a program on ETA, he greeted his father, saying, 'Good morning, Daddy.' Nnamdi was a carbon copy of Mr Udomu, who was tall and dark in complexion, in contrast to Stella, who was fair and average in height. Nnamdi had done well at the secondary school and had applied to one of the best universities in the country. He was waiting for his letter of admission.

'Where is your brother?' Mr Udomu asked, flicking his fingers impatiently. 'He is still sleeping,' Nnamdi answered. Mr Udomu's eyes gleamed angrily. 'Stella!' he shouted. Stella walked his position. 'It is seven o'clock, yet Vincent is still in bed,' he said.

'If you are so familiar with his actions, I see no reason why I should get him up every morning. He is old enough to do that himself,' Stella said steadily and stepped towards the bedroom.

'No, Stella. Is that all you have to say?'

Mr Udomu dropped his briefcase and hurried to Vincent's room on hearing him cough. Vincent was coughing seriously and had difficulty breathing. 'I think your cough is the result of the breeze and rain yesterday,' Mr Udomu said, watching Vincent shiver. His eyebrows wrinkled with worry.

'I'm sorry, Daddy,' Vincent said, slightly hoarse.

'I will give you some money to get yourself cough syrup,' Udomu said. His hand went to his pocket, and he brought out a clean note of money and handed it to Vincent. Udomu assured Vincent that he would be back from work before his usual time.

Minutes later, Vincent came out of his room, dressed in his white T-shirt and faded green trousers with a white hat pulled down to his nose. He walked to the table and ate his breakfast. 'Mummy, I would like to go buy myself cough syrup,' he said as he walked past his mum. 'Vincent!' she called without looking his way.

'Yes, Mum?'

'If I yell at you now, that won't make you happy, right? Punishing you wouldn't do either,' Stella said simply. 'I just want you to be sensible and be good. I won't tell you this a second time. Drugs make one utterly useless in society. Go get the medicine, and don't be long,' she added.

Vincent walked on a foot path towards a pharmacist; he turned when he heard Sule's voice shouting his name, and he hastily shifted his eyes. 'Where to?' Sule asked.

'I want to buy cough syrup at the pharmacist's.' Vincent answered, pointing in the direction of the shop.

Sule's eyebrows went up, and he started to laugh. 'I told you that you are your father's shadow,' he said.

'How do you mean?'

'You take syrups; I also take them, and I wouldn't mind if you bought me one,' Sule said sharply.

Vincent coughed and began to ruffle his T-shirt with the palm of his hand. 'What does it do?'

'Each time I take cough syrup, I feel a unique confidence and boldness, and it increases my desire to smoke more cigarettes,' Sule explained.

'Are you sure about that?' Vincent asked.

'I'm sure. You can experiment with it.'

'Okay, I will try that.'

The two boys walked to the pharmacy. Vincent bought two bottles of Benylin with codeine and handed one to Sule, and they walked back to the path. Vincent looked up and saw a girl coming, facing them on the path. He could hardly believe his eyes; she looked so beautiful in a short, red gown which clung to her figure. Her hair was loose, falling to her shoulders, and her make-up was flawless and provocative. Vincent thought she looked like a high-class movie star.

They moved closer. Vincent caught the scent of sweet perfume. He felt a little dazed, as if he were experiencing a magnificent dream. He was surprised when Sule started to smile. 'Rose!' He called.

'Yeah, Sule,' Rose answered, smiling.

'How are you?' Vincent said, moving to the other path so that he could watch her face. He saw a very lovely little girl.

Rose blushed. 'Oh, I'm fine . . .' she said 'Maybe I'd better go.' She turned away from Sule.

'Where to?' Sule asked.

'To get the usual stuff, of course.' Vincent looked at her going towards the pharmacist and then shifted his eyes back to his friend.

'She looked good!' he said.

'Never think a girl is suitable by her looks without knowing the sort of life she lives,' Sule said, following Vincent down the narrow path. 'Rose is so bad that most of her companions get into trouble because of her. It wouldn't be as bad if she only requested a lot of alcohol, cough syrup or cigarettes like we do, but she also steals from her friends and talks her way out of it even when caught. She doesn't care about people's opinion of her.'

Vincent turned back and watched Rose. *It makes no difference*, he thought with a cigarette between his thin lips.

'You haven't told me why you did not go to school today,' Sule said.

'I felt quite cold after the rain yesterday, and I began to cough this morning,' Vincent answered. 'I'd better go. My mummy warned me to come back on time,' he added and walked toward his house.

He went over and opened the door, glancing up and catching his reflection in the shiny door. He looked at himself and adjusted the sleeves of his T-shirt.

'If I were you,' Nnamdi said seriously, 'I would think it is un-necessary to break the rules with cigarettes. It's better to settle down for good grades instead.'

Vincent turned Nnamdi's direction in the sitting room and stared at him for a while. 'I think that sounds smart, but to hell with that for an idea for my life,' he said finally and went into his room.

Vincent took the wrapper off the bottle with his teeth and carefully raised it to his mouth; he took a long pull and blinked. 'Hey!' he shouted sharply as he finished the syrup and felt drowsy. He lay on the mattress and lit a cigarette; his eyes swam mistily as he smoked one cigarette after another and finally dozed off.

Mr Udomu came back from his office a few minutes before his usual time; he went straight into Vincent's room and found an empty bottle of Benylin and three cigarette butts on the floor. 'No, I won't take this! Abusing cough syrup?' he said loudly. He carefully watched Vincent on the mattress for a moment and then left the room, slamming the door behind himself.

The next day in the morning, with the sun beating down on the city, Vincent left the flat and moved towards the car. He held his head down and slowly shuffled his feet in the sand as he stood beside the car, waiting for his father. Minutes later, Mr Udomu came out of the flat. He stepped towards the car and jerked the door open, and Vincent joined him inside. 'Vincent, I thought I was making things easier for you by understanding that you like cigarettes. But I won't watch you taking cough syrup for no reason! I believe you can get the feeling you want without going this far.'

'I'm sorry, Dad. I will try to change,' Vincent replied. He got out of the car on reaching the school and ran into the building.

I have to be careful now that Daddy found out that I abuse cough syrup, he thought the next day, walking towards a pharmacy. 'I need a bottle of Benylin,' Vincent said once he was at the shop. A short, fat man who owned the pharmacy walked to the white counter and handed him a bottle of cough syrup. Vincent paid the man and put the medicine in his trouser pocket. He walked home majestically. Vincent went into his room and thought of hanging around outside. He slowly left the flat.

Nnamdi sat on the edge of a plastic chair under a small canopy, enjoying nature and staring at Vincent. *Suppose he says no to abusing drugs. Will it make him crazy?* Nnamdi thought.

Vincent felt dull and wanted a cigarette badly. He put his hand into his trouser pocket, brought out a bottle of cough syrup, and sipped from it. Nnamdi went to the door and then turned, saying, 'Be careful, little brother. It seems you don't really plan to change.'

Vincent didn't look concerned at this. He walked behind the flat and lit a cigarette. He realized in few minutes that he had smoked five cigarettes, which he had never done before at one time. He felt happy. 'This is good,' he said, and he rose to his feet abruptly and entered the flat again.

Chapter Four

Vincent in University

———⊖ ⊖———

Mr Udomu was shaving in his beautifully furnished bathroom. Outside, the wind and rain lashed the walls of the house, making it shudder and forcing Stella to shout a little as she talked to Mr Udomu about her missing money.

'The large amount of currency I had, about eight thousand naira, has become seven thousand naira,' she said.

Mr Udomu, who was half-dressed, held his shaving brush suspended, halfway to his face. 'I don't get it!' he said. Stella smiled with a look that certainly had a hint of come-hither intent.

'My money is missing.'

Mr Udomu tilted his head and frowned. 'You can't be serious, can you? There has been no theft in this house before. Why now?'

'I suspect your naughty son,' she said.

Mr Udomu put down his shaving brush and said, 'Suppose you ask and he did not take the money. How will he feel?'

'Who else would have done it? I couldn't possibly have done it myself, and I know you didn't.'

'Please, woman, stop making a mountain out of a molehill. I don't believe he did,' he replied. Stella said nothing but went to Vincent's room.

'Where is the money you took from my purse?' she demanded. Vincent, who lay staring at the rose-pink lanterns in his room, turned her way.

'I never took your money, Mother.'

'How can I believe that? Who else could have done it, if not you?' Vincent turned over to the other side of the mattress without any further answer.

The evening was a bit cold. Vincent walked onto the veranda in a corner of the flat and sat down, wearing a soft hat carelessly. A cigarette dangled from the side of his mouth, and his black eyes looked like bits of glass staring at the wall; he took a little bottle out of his pocket and fondled it. 'I knew it would,' he said with a thin grimace. But it was a good thing he didn't look too closely; the bottle was empty. 'Not again!! Making the same mistake twice; I shouldn't have put the empty bottle into my pocket.'

Vincent never thought there was anything wrong with taking a bottle of cough syrup that contained codeine and smoking a good number of cigarettes before he brushed his teeth for breakfast every morning. This continued throughout his secondary-school days.

He stole a good amount of money from the mother and father's pockets without being caught.

He was admitted into a university with average grades and moved into the student hostel. Vincent walked towards the school garden, a place with many trees, some which were heavy with fruit. He saw a girl wearing an extremely tight-fitting yellow gown.

The gown had a high neckline and long sleeves, and it swept the floor gracefully. The girl wore a large, white bow in her hair which matched with the sandals on her feet.

A tall man walked up to the girl and started chatting, preventing Vincent from seeing as much of her as he wished. By leaning forward, Vincent could see her head; by leaning back, he could just see her gown on the floor. He wished the tall man would go away. He moved a little closer and recognized the girl Sule had condemned. 'Hi, Rose! How do you do?'

'Pretty good.' Rose answered, wondering where she had met him. His face looked familiar.

'Please excuse me.' Vincent leant forward and removed an invisible hair from Rose's gown. The tall guy gave him a searching look.

'Sorry, mister, have we met somewhere?' she asked pleasantly.

'I am Vincent, Sule's friend,' he answered.

'Oh yeah. How are you? Do you go to school here?'

'Yeah, although this is my first year in the university,' Vincent answered. They started chatting about the school rules of discipline, and Rose told him the best place to smoke without being caught.

The subject did not interest the tall guy. 'Please excuse us,' he said. Vincent watched them go rather sadly and went into class, looking at his wristwatch and said, 'It is time already.'

The Lecturer for the Introduction to Entrepreneurship course came into the classroom very quickly, and a smile lit his face as he noticed the students were all waiting seriously. Vincent listened to the lecturer without enthusiasm; he felt the day was a complete flop. 'You!' said the lecturer, pointing in Vincent's direction. 'I've just said that enterprises are defined in two contexts: the wider context and the narrower context. Tell me the narrower context.' Vincent looked around the class. 'I mean you, Vincent Udomu,' the man shouted.

'No idea, sir.' A ripple of laughter passed through the class.

'I'm afraid you are a very dull boy.' The lecturer turned to another boy who raised his hand on hearing the question. 'Yes?'

'The meaning of enterprise in a narrower context is simply a business venture or an undertaking that brings profit.'

'Very good; now, class, get ready to take a test during my next lecture hour,' the lecturer added and walked out of the class. Vincent walked out of the classroom and buried his head in the sand regarding the test.

Bright sunlight filtered through a window high on the wall of the hostel. Vincent sat on the edge of his bed, his mood as bright as the sunshine as he thought of his brief encounter with Rose. *I know I can at least get a bottle of a cough syrup from her*, he thought.

He left his room and made his way to an open space close to a farm behind the school. He found Rose and three young men standing under a tree, smoking cigarettes and wrapped marijuana. Rose handed Vincent a cigarette. 'This is the best place to enjoy any spare time, and no one will know what you've taken or smoked. Please excuse me; I need to buy myself a bottle of cough syrup,' she added.

'Can I come with you?'

'Why not? Suit yourself,' Rose said, glancing over at Vincent, and they made their way to a pharmacy.

Later, Vincent walked to his bunk and quickly drank the syrup. He lay on the mattress at last. As he looked at the empty bottle, his expression was like someone who is constantly drunk. Before he dozed off, he thought aloud in penetrating tones about the test he was supposed to take.

Chapter Five

A Journey of Dishonour

⸺◦ ◦⸺

Vincent stayed in bed late, and then he suddenly walked to the window, sliding the curtains aside. The sunlight came through the slats in the shutter and burnt his feet.

He scratched his head, yawned and then reached under the bed for his slippers. He sat there, staring outside and feeling lousy. Vincent pressed his fingers tenderly to his head. *I have missed the test, but I will read for his next exam and surprise that good-for-nothing lecturer,* he thought *Yes!* He got dressed. He looked at himself as he stood before a mirror and forgot what he had thought of earlier; all he could think about was how to get a cough syrup and cigarettes.

As soon as he was outside, Vincent glanced up and down a path that led out of the hostel. He walked to the grounds behind the hostel; they stretched away to the waterfront, and he saw the flowers, trees, palms and everything that grew so richly in the tropical heat spread out before him. He reached the smoking area and stood, looking for a stone to sit on.

He had only been standing there for a few minutes when a tall, distinguished-looking guy holding an elaborate leather folder approached him and said, 'You are just the guy I was looking for.'

Vincent gave him a quick, puzzled glance. 'Who are you, and why are you looking for me?' he asked.

'I'm surprised you don't recognize me," the guy said, now looking puzzled himself. 'Anyway, I'm Musa. I was one of the guys standing with Rose yesterday,' he added.

'Oh, yeah! Please don't mind me. You looked so familiar, but I forgot where we had met,' Vincent said, adjusting his stance.

'Whether you like what I want to tell you will depend on your interests,' Musa started. 'There's a fine show at Hip Spot. You ought to see it. I went last year and would love to stay there permanently. Vincent hastily shifted his eyes. He was so confused that he pulled out his handkerchief and wiped his sweaty hands.

'I don't get you.'

'Hip Spot is just eighty kilometres away from this city, and there is so much entertainment going on, a lot of the normal stuff for adults. People are very amused. I've seen a lot of that kind of stuff, but this is the best. Take my word: you ought not to miss it,' Musa said and tapped the ash from his cigarette.

'How can one get there?' Vincent asked.

'I can let you have a ticket if you fancy it.' Musa bowed his head as he tore a slip of paper and then handed it to Vincent. 'Fill this out; it serves as your ticket. This might be different from any of the parties you have been to.'

Vincent looked at the date; it was the same day he would be starting the first-semester examinations. 'What happens if I miss an examination at this school?' he asked.

'Nothing much. You just have to retake the course next session,' Musa said. 'But you won't miss much. The show is just for two days, and then we will be back. Someone with an odd name went with us last semester; I've forgotten his real name. He had to resit but passed it later on. I used to see him whenever I went to his department, but he was a cold, hard-faced guy; that made me play around with the idea of kicking him out of my circle of friends.'

Days passed, and the school library was filled with lots of students as the examination period approached. Vincent also went to the school library to study, but he never read for the first two courses that he thought would be carried over to the next semester.

On 27 March of that year, Vincent woke up as the small, ornate clock on the mantelpiece struck four o'clock in the morning and got dressed. He walked out of his bunk quickly and impatiently.

After about five minutes, Vincent arrived behind a gas station, where Rose and three boys were waiting. Musa's face brightened as Vincent said, 'Hi, guys.'

'Get in. We're short on time for the journey.' Vincent and two of the boys rushed into the back seat of the car. Rose jumped into the passenger seat, and Musa got into the driver's seat and started the engine. 'Take it easy, man; the first seven kilometres are the worst,' Musa added before he drove for some time in the darkness, and then he swung off the highway and onto a bad road.

When he had gone several kilometres, he considered it safe enough to stop as the day was brightened by the morning's subdued sun. He opened the window and put his head through the opening. 'Rose, it's time for breakfast. Share the stuff.' Rose handed each person a bottle of cough syrup and two cigarettes. They enjoyed the stuff for a while silently and then drove off.

Three days later, Vincent came back to the hostel; he turned the door handle and went in. His roommate, Oke, jumped away from the door. 'You scared me, Vincent,' he said.

'I'm sorry to come barging in on you like this,' Vincent said, standing just inside the room and still holding the door handle.

'That's all right. But wait a moment; is it true you travelled with those dropout guys?' Oke asked.

'Dropout guys?' Vincent repeated impartially. He came further into the room and shut the door.

'Maybe I should introduce them to you properly. Musa and those guys and Rose dropped out of this university, and they are drug slaves. Everyone in this institution knows them, and I'm very sorry that you value them as friends to the point of missing two examinations,' Oke said very bitterly.

'I will make it up!' Vincent assured himself and Oke, dropping his small bag on the mattress.

Vincent took the rest of his examinations without enthusiasm. All he thought was having more experiences like he'd had at the Hip Spot.

The semester soon ended, and the second semester began. Every student came to check his or her grade during the first week. Vincent's name was among the expelled students. 'To hell!' he said and sadly went back home.

'Why back so soon?' the mum asked.

'The school has expelled me,' He confidently answered and then dropped his eyes. There was a long pause.

'This is the consequence of drug abuse!' she said, sounding so miserable.

The next day, Mr Udomu called Vincent, who was sitting in the corridor, smoking wrapped marijuana. 'I'm so disappointed,' he said. Vincent bowed.

'I am exceedingly sorry, Dad.'

'Now, I want you to stop abusing drugs. I mean not even smoking a cigarette in this house.'

'I'm afraid I can't agree to that,' Vincent answered and walked out of Mr Udomu and Stella's presence, leaving them both wearing angry expressions.

'You will have to come up with a plan to help him before it gets worst,' Stella said. Mr Udomu sadly walked out and took up a position by the door, murmuring about how much freedom he allowed his son and gave a harsh little laugh.

The following morning, Mr Udomu sat in the driver's seat of his car and sent the gatekeeper to call his son. In less than fifteen minutes, Vincent walked towards his father rather gingerly. Mr Udomu looked at him closely and asked, 'Are you drunk this early?'

Vincent shook his head. 'I am just a little sleepy this morning,' he said.

'Anyway, I would like you to join me at my office to get a message for your mother,' he said.

'You think it is necessary for me to go with you instead of your office driver?' Vincent asked.

'I don't trust the driver for a second,' Mr Udomu said seriously.

'Very well, then. I will do exactly as you suggest.' He staggered to the passenger seat, and Mr Udomu drove at an incredible speed to a big building and honked his horn in the middle of the big compound.

'I'm sorry, Son; I did not teach you good discipline so you could learn the good side of life.' He seemed to lose control of himself on seeing two men coming towards them, but he wiped the tears that fell from his eyelashes with his handkerchief and said, 'Starting today, I'm going to miss you as a result of my lack of discipline for you at a tender age. I regret that your present substance abuse is a result of my negligence to raise you up properly.' He turned toward the men. 'These are staff of the National Drug Law Enforcement Agency,' he tearfully added. One of the men jerked the car door open and asked Vincent to step out. Moments later, Vincent watched his father slowly driving out of the office compound in tears.

Three months later, Vincent was fully rehabilitated and reintegrated into the society. He had since started his education all over again.

Part II

Chapter One

The School

———⌒　⌒———

It was a new session at Brilliant Boys College. The students assembled, each wearing neat purple trousers and a white, long-sleeved shirt with a purple tie and deerskin shoes.

'Good morning, sir,' said the students.

'How are you today?' asked Mr Oshevire, who stood facing the students on a high, cement platform.

'Pretty good, sir,' the students answered.

'As you are all aware, Brilliant Boys College is a school of excellence and discipline. I am warning you not to be involved in any form of drug abuse or bad behaviour. Any student caught gives the school a bad image; have I made myself clear?'

'Yes, sir!'

'I wish you all the best this term,' the principal said in conclusion. As he made his way down the steps, the students silently marched into their classes.

The students murmured about Mr Oshevire's disciplinary measures and unsmiling behaviour. William, sitting at the second desk in the third row, watched as most of the students talked and a few were silent. He wondered what sort of a life he would lead. The bell brought his attention back to the class. *All the students are leaving with their friends, and here I am, all by myself,* he thought and suddenly stood up. William walked down a path that led to a woman who sells food with his hands in his pocket. He turned to his left and saw some boys afar; they were almost hidden by the bushes.

One of the boys brought out a pack of cigarettes and weed already wrapped in Rizla paper; each of the boys collected a cigarette quickly. He watched them walking towards the rock. 'What are they up to?' he whispered as he followed the boys slowly. He hid and watched the boys light their cigarettes. 'What joy could they be deriving from it?' William wondered. Then he made a quick, silent detour and walked towards them, pretending not to notice them.

His sudden appearance triggered fear in the boys. They looked as if they were going to spring to their feet, but seeing that he was so close, they quickly threw the cigarettes into the bushes and turned away as if they hadn't see him. William felt it would be safe to approach the boys. 'Hi guys!' he said.

Sani, the tallest among the boys, stared straight into his eyes. The expression that crossed his face made him look old and ugly. 'Yes, how may we help you?' he asked harshly. His voice scared William deeply, and he quickly moved a step away.

'Eh . . . !'

'Listen, don't you dare say a word to the principal or anyone. These and other drugs make us happy; without them we are lost in the dark part of life,' Sani said, and he made a sign to the rest of boys. William watched them with his mouth agape as they walked past him. Although they looked shabby, there was a rhythmic smartness in their movements.

The following morning, William walked into his class on the ground floor of the first building and sat down comfortably. He stretched his legs beneath the huge mahogany desk and glanced at the guy sitting next to him.

He recognized one of the boys he saw smoking behind a rock the day before and wondered why he looked so sad. 'How are you today?' he asked, striking up a conversation. Sani looked back at him for a while without saying a word. *Maybe he likes straight shooters, and fancy language bothers him*, William thought. 'I played around with the idea of getting to know why you guys take drugs,' he said.

'Shut your beastly mouth! I told you not to say anything about what you saw,' Sani replied. William noticed that he had suddenly gone very pale and had difficulty controlling himself.

'I'm sorry!' he said, looking at Sani calmly.

'Just do yourself a favour by never saying a word about it in class,' Sani whispered as Mrs Lydia entered the classroom.

'Luke!' she called at the end of the teaching. 'Bring everyone's assignment books to my table in about ten minutes from now!'

'Yes, ma'am,' Luke answered. Sani watched until she had disappeared. Then he stood and elaborately walked out of the class, without giving the class rep his assignment, as if he had just noticed the door.

William stood very still over a woman who sold biscuits and crackers on small table under a tree during the short break. 'Madam, I need a cream cracker,' he demanded and then paused when he felt a hand on his shoulder. William quickly turned and saw Sani. He was frightened and surprised. 'I'm damn sorry I ever hurt you!' he said.

'I'm not as unpleasant of a person as you thought. I would like to talk with you,' Sani said and walked towards the rock.

Sani continued. 'You saw me smoking a cigarette and probably marijuana yesterday. That's what makes me feel nervous. I'm already addicted to drugs, and there is nothing anyone can do about that; I'm saying this for you to keep your mouth shut,' Sani warned.

'I would like to experience the excitement you feel after taking drugs.'

Sani looked at him curiously and laughed at him. 'I started taking drugs from Buba, out of ignorance. He lived a mile away from my house, so we walked home together after school. I always saw him take cigarettes and not get tired because of them. One day I asked for a cigarette, which I smoked and felt excited and strong. Since then, living without drugs feels like the creator took away the beautiful world and gave me an ugly one instead. I smoke both cigarettes and marijuana, just as Buba does,' Sani said indistinctly. 'Now I am addicted.'

'You've said that already!' William interrupted with a blank look on his face. 'I would like to taste it.' Sani laughed again. William frowned. He didn't like Sani's hissing little laugh so close to his ear. 'What's so funny about it?'

'Frankly, I think you are about to take the most damnable risk,' he answered.

'You scared the life out of me in class earlier,' William said, changing the topic of conversation. 'It made me think you were a tough bird.

Sani laughed, shaking his head. 'You're a wise kid.'

William looked at him intently. 'Really, why shouldn't I?

'I do a lot of nasty things when I'm on drugs; I might fight and take someone's property or even steal from myself unknowingly.

There was a long, uneasy paused as they heard a strange sound in the bushes and suddenly gazed at each other with their mouths open. Sani quickly threw the cigarette into the bush, falling silent as the sound increased. 'Come with me,' he whispered. They got quietly to their feet and rushed to the other side of the rock. Sani peeped through a gap between the rocks. He saw a big rat and drew a deep breath. 'It's a rat,' he told William, so they walked back to the place they were earlier.

The appearance of Ali, Buba, and Zubo made Sani panic, as he was taking marijuana. William stood over Sani, watching the way he was taking the drug, and he also panicked. The new arrivals gave a sudden squeal of laughter on seeing how Sani tried to spring to his feet.

'What is he here for?' Buba asked, referring to William. He looked puzzled.

'He is a harmless guy, and we are now friends.

Buba's face lit up, and he shook William's hand feverishly. 'My legs were almost too weak to support my body, and my shirt stuck to my back as I sweated profusely with fear of seeing the person who caught us last time.' He looked at Sani for a while but continued speaking to William. 'I'm working hard to trust what Sani says about you, because I've got a lot of confidence in him. You must not disappoint us by putting us in the hands of the school authorities.

'Sure!' William answered, nodding his head. There was a long, strained silence. William stood over the boys, watching them light their cigarettes.

William is the only son of Mr Odibo, the principal of Kings High School. Mr Odibo was a soft-spoken, patient sort of man who wanted the best educational reputation for his only son.

William's eyes swept over the boys and came to rest on Sani, and he wondered about Sani's personality, which was so strong that he made the rest of the boys, including Buba, seem like mere paintings on the wall. *He is tall with big, powerful shoulders, tapering away to a small waist and very long legs. I think he is the leader of this group.* William thought.

The bell rang, and the boys quickly hid the marijuana and then hurried to their classes. Their faces were straight, as if they were doing nothing wrong. William thought they were good actors.

Chapter Two

Escape of the Bad Boys

The topic of conversation between Sani and the three other boys was entirely about the excitement they felt after taking marijuana. 'I find things very dull without drugs,' Sani said. William, who was given some good stuff to try, looked at him sharply.

'I heard that Mrs Lydia rescheduled the test we were supposed to take tomorrow to the fifth of next month,' Zubo said.

'I have tried to discover who Zubo is without success. He is talkative, but he steers the conversation away from any personal topic,' Sani said. They all laughed hysterically.

William tried a little of the marijuana. He smiled brightly and put it down with a little shudder. 'Yeah!' he exclaimed.

'You like it?' Sani asked anxiously, looking at him closely.

'It's like nothing I've ever tasted before; I wouldn't say I liked it, but I want it.'

'Poor little William. I'm sure you're feeling a lot right now,' Buba said, smiling.

'Yes, I feel that I had something new. I can tell I feel very happy right now.' He reached for a cigarette. He lit the cigarette. Sani watched him for a while and raised his hand to stop William from striking a match for the second time.

'That will be enough for you, man!' he advised. William was too dazed to speak; he lay limply on the low grasses. 'It seems your head is on fire. It is always like this the first time.' Sani knelt down beside him.

'He is not going with us. He will implicate us if he does,' Buba declared.

'But how could you think that we would leave him here?'

'Have you forgotten the risk I took the first day Zubo joined us. I thought I knew what I was doing; at least I know Zubo could get me into trouble,' Buba explained. 'We will have to check on him in about half an hour. The experience of that afternoon makes me think it is pointless to be around William at the moment.

William, whose eyes were half-closed, suddenly became conscious that something awful had happened to him, but he hadn't the strength to stand to his feet. The boys walked past him. William struggled up and fell back to the ground. 'Rest, man! We will be back for you,' Sani said and followed closely behind the other boys. The news of students who took drugs behind a rock soon reached Mr Oshevire. 'I saw a boy lying beside a rock very close to the school; I saw at a glance that he was a little drunk,' reported Nathan, one of the school teachers, as he stood before the principal.

'Get the security officers and fetch him at once,' Mr Oshevire said. Nathan walked to the school gate and repeated what he saw and the principal's message to the security guards, and they followed him.

Sani rushed out of geography class when it ended. He walked over to where William was near the rock. 'Hi! Wake up! You must be strong enough now,' he said, hitting William's shoulder.

William turned his way. 'Where are your unpleasant friends?' William asked abruptly.

'I think it's not time for us to talk about that. Come on! Let's get out of here.' Sani struggled. They slowly moved towards the edge of the building and hid behind a large flower pot on seeing Nathan and two security guards passing through the building, taking the path towards the rock. William and Sani watched the men until they were out of sight, and then they walked into the classroom. Sani held William's arm pretending he was horribly sick.

Nathan supervised the search around the rock, but they didn't find any students. He ran his fingers through his thin hair, and his eyes grew very wide. 'Oh no . . . no . . . he escaped,' he said, and they walked back to the principal's office. 'He's gone; I mean, he escaped, sir,' Nathan said.

Mr Oshevire looked at him, trying hard to hide the anger in his eyes. He stopped his breath from rattling in his throat. 'Perhaps you wanted that to happen.'

'No, sir!' he replied.

'Don't be nervous, Nathan. You knew that the boy might escape, yet you told me without evidence.'

'I'm sorry.'

'I want you to organize a search group. You must find the students who are involved in drug abuse, right?

'Yes, sir. I will do just that,' Nathan answered and made his way out of the principal's office.

The school's closing bell rang at about fifteen minutes to two. William walked towards a red Honda Civic and settled himself in the front seat. The driver looked at him for a while, noticing his eyes were quite red. William, who had expected that, shifted his head a trifle. The driver smiled and shifted gears.

The driver wanted to know the fullest details about William's decision. 'Isn't it a pity that you're living this sort of life?' he asked.

'How do you mean?' William gave him a sharp look.

'I can tell you are on drugs, and it will do you no good,' the driver advised.

'I feel excited now that I'm on drugs. If not for the feeling, I would give it up,' William answered.

'That is a good reason to take drugs, but there are other ways to be happy.'

'Those ways are very difficult for me,' William said.

On reaching number six, Zebra Close, Fatima Estate, the driver honked the horn, and the gate opened. He drove into the compound and came to a halt in the front of the flat. He shook his head as he watched William climbing the stairs gingerly. William opened his door, dragged himself onto the bed, and kicked the door shut. He noticed that it was very hot in the room even though the shutters kept out the sun.

He walked out of the room and out the front door slowly. 'Hey!' he called out to the driver.

'I took drugs, but don't you dare a word about that to my father,' he warned the driver, looking at him sharply again. He walked back to the flat with a grimace. *Yes! I know I have scared the life out of him the way Sani did to me in the class the other day*, he thought.

Chapter Three

The School Authorities

Time passed fairly quickly as the boys continued going to the rock between the school and the teachers' quarters for several weeks without being caught. 'Guys, let me have your money for tomorrow,' Buba said. 'I can't contribute today because I'm tight for money right now,' he continued awkwardly. William pulled a wallet from his hip pocket and brought out a thousand-naira note. He stood looking at the note for moment, and then he closed his fingers around it tightly and handed it to Buba, saying "I think we all should intensify effort in sourcing for money", sighing at the same time.

Buba collected the other boys' money and sat down on the grass. 'William,' he called, looking at him suspiciously. 'I guess I am the boss of this group because I introduced most of you, and we've gotten along so far, haven't we, Sani?' Sani did not say anything. He shifted uncomfortably. 'I consider myself humble, but you have a prideful attitude just because I'm tight for money this week. You should be careful not to insult me!'

'How dare you address me that way, you great oaf?' William replied.

Buba considered starting a fight but decided that it would only get him in trouble with Sani. All the same, his fingers itched to get a grip on William' thin neck, but he simply ignored him, and that certainly affected William.

Sani smiled bitterly, exposing his piano-like teeth. 'I hope I did not make a great mistake to regard you as a friend. I don't care who gave you a lot of money, and it doesn't matter how much trouble you had to get such an amount. You've got to leave it outside. Lots of money and fancy words aren't going to help us. Do you understand? He said harshly, looking at William's clouded face.

'Yeah, but he had to contribute. This is the third time now he hadn't.

'Listen!' Sani interrupted. 'I know when Buba has money. So you shut your mouth this minute.'

William said nothing, but he rolled his eyes a little. 'I'm sorry man!' Sani said as he turned and put his hands on Buba's shoulders.

Nathan and two security guards walked quietly towards the rock. They saw a number of boys smoking marijuana. The two security officers crouched down and crawled to a spot where they felt it possible to reach the boys. They jumped on the boys and caught Buba and Zubo. Nathan caught Ali after a good chase. 'I have taken part in several competitions, attained a record speed, and kept to it for six months, you bitch,' said Nathan, who looked thin and fairly old. He held Ali very tightly. Ali was completely powerless in Nathan's grip.

Two more security men rushed over. One of the men tied Ali's hands tightly behind his back and went towards the principal's office. Nathan and the other security guard started to run along the path that Sani and William took. They ran past a flat very close to a stream.

Mr John moved to his new flat a week ago. He left the door open, but now it is locked. Those boys may have gone into the house to hide, he thought and called the attention of the security guard. They went over to the old flat and knocked on the door, and it was locked from the inside. 'I know you are in there, you oafs!' Nathan shouted. There was silence. He moved uneasily and peeked through a gap between the wooden window slats. Nathan saw William trembling in fear. 'I have you. Just come out of the building to save yourself trouble,' he shouted.

Evening was drawing on rapidly, and the sun, wrapped in a haze, was sinking below the horizon. Sani and William remained in the old flat. Sani, who hid under an old table, came out to stretch his legs, and William followed his example.

They both peeped through the narrow gaps in the window and saw Nathan and two security guards waiting at the door; Sani moved and saw that there were other security officers standing against each window outside the flat. 'We will have to give up. I'm sorry. Escaping is quite impossible,' Sani said. William got more scared and worried. 'We've lost the fight,' Sani continued, walking towards the door.

'Don't you dare touch it!' William shouted.

'Don't talk to me in that tone again. However, I can't expect you to understand that we have lost the battle.' William ran to one of the rooms and tried to protect himself with upraised arms as Sani opened the door and a security man walked in. 'I'm sorry, sir,' he cried out.

At the same time, he heard Nathan bark, 'Seize him!'

'Shut up,' said a security guard to Sani.

William crouched against the wall, weeping softly, as another security officer came closer. He tied his hands behind William's back and joined Nathan and the other guards outside the flat.

They walked towards the principal's house, which was a few kilometres away from the school. 'Nathan, you've made me proud,' said the principal. He turned to the security guards and said, 'Take them to the police station until tomorrow and inform their parents; they must be punished.'

'Yes, sir,' the four security men answered and made their way to the station.

Mr Odibo came home a few minutes past six o'clock, and he saw the driver in the car outside the compound. 'Shehu,' he called, 'why are you outside?

'Oga, I just came from Brilliant Boys College. William is nowhere to be found.'

'What do you mean my son is nowhere to be found? Did you go to the school early?' he asked anxiously.

'Yes, sir, and I waited until a few minutes ago.'

'We have to go back and look for him.'

Mr Odibo jerked the car door open. He settled himself into a corner of the back seat; the driver watched him in the mirror and saw horror in his eyes. Mr Odibo pulled out his handkerchief and wiped his sweaty face. They drove for some time on a dirt road and then swung off to the highway. Mr Odibo jumped from the car quickly as they came to a halt before the school gate, and he rushed up to the security officers. 'I'm looking for my son, William

Odibo; my driver told me he brought him to school this morning.'

'Oga,' one of the security guards replied, 'we don't know any boy bearing such name. The teachers and principal keep track of students' names. However, some boys were caught a few minutes ago and were taken to the principal's house,' he explained.

'Please, can you show me where the principal's house is?' Mr Odibo asked anxiously.

The first security guard replied, 'Bello can. His shift is almost over, so we can spare him.'

Mr Odibo turned and asked, 'Bello, can you help me?'

'Yes, just a minute,' Bello said and went into a small room near the main gate of the school. Mr Odibo shifted restlessly. Bello soon appeared, and they walked towards the car.

As Bello directed them, the driver took a turn at the end of the street and then kept going straight on the road to the principal's house.

'Good evening, sir,' Mr Odibo, said shaking the principal's hand when they arrived. 'I'm Mr Odibo. Please, I'm looking for William Odibo, one of your students in Senior Secondary Class 1.

'Oh! I sent him away with the security guards. He's at the police station by now.'

'Police station?' Mr Odibo asked.

'Yes, he was caught smoking marijuana when he should have been in class.'

'What?'

'I'm sorry. You can see your son when you report to the school tomorrow.'

'Thank you,' Mr Odibo said sadly.

The driver glimpsed an expression in his employer's eyes that told him Mr Odibo was in a very bad shape, terrified almost as if he were a child awakening from an evil nightmare. 'Sir, I wanted to speak to you about William's drug habit, but he warned me not to say a word. He said he would kill me if I did.'

William, William, what have I not done to make you happy? I wish your mother was still with me. Now that she has left, you have a lot of freedom, Mr Odibo thought. He briefly lost control of himself but wiped the tears that clung to his eyelashes with the tip of a handkerchief as the driver drove him home.

Chapter Four

Disappointments

———⊖ ⊖———

Mr Oshevire called for an assembly the following morning and asked the security guards to take the boys caught smoking to the assembly ground. 'As the principal of Brilliant Boys College, it is my responsibility to help you be your best; some of the foolish ones among you thought it was a good idea to smoke all kinds of drugs, which leads to nasty behaviour inside and outside of school.

'Today, here are some fools who failed to consider their future. I want to get their names down on paper as bad, troublesome boys, and you all get to witness how their behaviour is treated,' the principal said, and he ordered the discipline master to whip each of the boys with twenty strokes from a cane. 'Don't miss a single stroke,' he added.

Mr Odibo watched the five boys wiping off their tears after the whipping as the principal wrote down their names. Before the assembly ended, the principal advised the rest of the students to take their studies seriously and warned them that a group would continue watching for drug use. Mr Odibo thanked the principal and left with William.

William came out of the flat days later; he was astonished to see Sani and the gatekeeper exchanging words. 'You no-good boy! William's father warned against people with your reputation visiting his son!' The gatekeeper sounded very serious.

'Let me in this minute, you oaf!'

'No! I mustn't let you any farther.'

'How long have you got to do this?'

'This is my classmate, Sani, a well-behaved boy,' William said as he walked up to his friend and the gatekeeper.

'I don't want to lose my job. I advise you to talk outside the compound.' The guard watched William make a gesture, and both boys walked out of the compound. 'By now, I thought he would get rid of such friends,' the gatekeeper said under his breath.

'My dad seemed to find the whole thing amusing, and he took a special interest in keeping me away from you guys. I take refuge in my room as much as possible with the excuse that I was studying,' William explained as they sat under a fruit tree a mile away from the flat.

'Where is he now?' Sani asked.

'He left to travel this morning. You know, money means so much to me. My father has cut back on the amount he gives me, William complained, pulling out a big wallet. He showed Sani a five-hundred-naira note. 'I am not pleased with him,' he added.

'Listen, I have every confidence that soon the storm will be over.' Sani smiled. 'Now I will let you in on my little secret. If your father doesn't give you enough money, get it yourself.' There was a tigerish look in his eyes as he spoke.

'Do you honestly mean to tell me that you have been doing that all this time?

'It is not as easy as you may think, but I have not tricked you, and there are many days to succeed before the storm.' William watched Sani with curiosity and said, 'I wonder who you really are.' Sani nodded in response.

'I resumed school yesterday,' Sani said. 'I wonder when your father will let you start instead of staying by yourself in the flat.'

'He transferred me to King High School, which I will be starting next week,' William said, looking guilty.

'I'm going to miss you a hell of a lot; I wish you were coming back. It hurts me to see you go after we formed a friendship which was altogether remarkable because we had something in common,' Sani cried.

'I found your company very exhilarating, which made me want to see a lot more of you.' Sani was pleased that William felt that way.

'Well, you know how things are right now, but I will try to visit you from time to time.' He shook William's hand sadly and walked away.

William soon resumed his education at King High School, and this time it was impossible for him to smoke cigarettes or weed, as Mr Odibo watched what he did every minute. One afternoon, William felt the need for company, so he walked to Mr Odibo's room. 'Daddy, can I sit by the gate to watch what's going on?' William asked.

Mr Odibo looked at him curiously. 'Don't you have anything to do, any assignments from school?'

'Yes, sir. I'm done with all my assignments.'

'All right then. Make sure you are careful!'

'Yes, Daddy,' he said and hurried over to Yusuf, who was sitting comfortably on a bench, leaning against the wall of a small building near the main gate. 'Hi?' William greeted Yusuf.

'Yes, how may I be of help to you?' William could see he was only giving him half his attention.

'I saw you and Anurika the other day smoking wrapped marijuana and drinking strong alcohol, and I wondered if that is what gives him a lot of strength.'

'Why do you want to know?' Yusuf asked suspiciously.

'I have tried it with my friends before, but we quarrelled and we went our separate ways. I want you men to constantly be my companions, as my father has confidence in you.'

'We take drugs secretly, so that no one suspects us. You must be a smart boy to do that.' Yusuf whispered, looking blankly at the flowers nearby.

'Trust me; I can be as smart as you are,' William replied.

'Here comes Anurika. Talk to him, and he will fix you up if you are as lucky as I am.' Yusuf smiled. Anurika walked over, and they spoke seriously. William was happy when Anurika invited him to a corner of the house and handed him a good quantity of marijuana.

'Can I also have something that sets fire to my blood?

'Smoke the weed first,' Anurika said.

'No, I'll taste the drink before I smoke anything!' William said. When he had tasted the drink, he put it down and struck a match to light a cigarette. Suddenly, they heard movement.

William quickly gave Anurika some money and collected a small bottle of Brandy and the marijuana.

He quickly put them into his trouser pocket and walked smartly into the flat through the front door.

A week later, William saw Anurika outside, fixing the generator. He ran to him. 'I have looked for you everywhere. My stuff is gone, and I need more.' William shuffled his feet in the sand. His eyes flinched, but his face looked stiff.

'I don't sell drugs. I only sold them to you the other day because I had enough and I needed money,' he said with a wolfish grin.

'You mean I can't get more from you?'

'I can only introduce you to my mother, who sells both alcohol and marijuana. Just be ready tomorrow, maybe when you get back from school,' Anurika said.

The next day, William and Anurika walked along the edge of a road which led to a curved path that lead to a very poor, shabby building, 'Sit here!' Anurika said, pointing to a wooden bench in the corner of the room. William first moved to the rough table standing in the middle of the room and looked at the picture of a woman hanging in a corner opposite the bench, and then he found a position on the bench.

'I guess that is your mother,' he said.

'Yes, she sells the drugs!' Anurika repeated as a distinguished woman in her late forties appeared.

'Do you want alcohol, marijuana, or cigarettes?' she asked.

'I prefer weed and alcohol.' William handed the woman a five hundred-naira note and looked at Anurika, who stood very still, his hands folded under his armpits. The woman soon returned with two bottles of alcohol and a good quantity of marijuana.

William put the drugs and the bottle of alcohol in his trouser pockets. 'I have to get going before my father starts to look for me,' he said.

'You must be careful.'

'Sure!' he said and ran out of the room, taking a path to his house.

That same afternoon, Mr Odibo went into his room; from the bathroom, he had noticed a small change in his bedroom: his wallet was open, and the shirt which had been on the bed was now on the floor. He carefully checked the wallet and found that a two-thousand-naira notes was missing. 'Who could possibly have been in my room?' he asked in frustration and stomped to William's room.

Mr Odibo started searching for his money on William's shelves. He saw something inside made of black leather, and he opened it and found a good quantity of Marijuana. 'Gee!' He continued the search and found lots of alcohol bottles under William's bed. Mr Odibo looked at the bottles with his mouth open in shock. 'Okaka,' he called, coming out to the sitting room. The door opened, and the tall, portly Okaka stepped into the well-furnished sitting room. 'Did you come to my room a while ago?

'No, sir. I've been by the gate since morning.'

'It's okay; I just wanted to be sure. You may go now,' Mr Odibo said.

Just then, William walked in, and he guessed why his father's face looked stern. His eyes revealed he felt scared because he was guilty. 'Give me the money. I know you want more alcohol instead of weed.

'Wow! How did he know?' William whispered. There was a long, uneasy pause. Mr Odibo shifted a little nearer, but William tried to keep a distance, rolling his bloodshot eyes a little.

'You thought I wouldn't find out?' he asked.

'I'm sorry, Daddy.' William cried, stepping away from Mr Odibo and past Okaka and then ran out of the compound.

Chapter Five

The Drug Slaves' Performance

———⋅ ⋅———

Sani graduated from Brilliant Boys College with fairly good results; he got admission into the department of accountancy at Falcon University.

'I've had a grand time. Maybe we will see each other later on,' he said to his friends as they staggered towards the hostel.

Falcon University was the biggest university in the state. The different departments were separated by yards with low grasses; the buildings contained many classes, and the offices were modern, with up-to-date learning materials. At the university, Sani made new friends who were also slaves to drugs. They met in an unfinished building very close to the accountancy department after the first lecture of the day. The young men tried to hide the drugs from him, but he brought out a cigarette and lit it. 'You smoke?' one of the young men said, sounding very surprised.

'Yeah.' Sani looked down, wiped his face with the back of his hand, and yawned.

'You look tired,' the young man said. 'Yes, that is why I'm drinking this,' Sani answered, bringing out a small bottle of alcohol; he took a nervous sip from it and rested against the wall for a while. He looked at the young men suspiciously. He felt tense until he walked out of the building. This continued for a long time, until one day, when Sani was sitting on a block in part of the uncompleted building, the other young men stepped toward him. Sani bowed his head, as usual. 'Hi, would you care for this?'

Sani raised his head and saw one of the young men wearing white trousers, a dark-red shirt, and sandals. Sani thought the young man looked extraordinarily handsome as he stood before him and smiled. 'Thank you, but how did you know I needed this?'

'We've watched you having this kind of drink for a long time now, even in the hostel,' the young man answered. It was a shock meeting him, as Sani couldn't remember ever seeing this young man. But Sani did not openly reveal his shock, and he became best of friends with these guys. When one of the group members wasn't careful enough, the rest kept him in line.

Days passed speedily. A new semester soon began, and during the first week, students walked to the notice board to check their results; some looked happy after checking, while some frowned and walked away without a word. Sani passed his classes with fair grades. But his friends' performances were so low that the university had no choice but to expel them.

'What could have caused such a failure after three years in school?' one of them cried.

Mallam Suleiman, Head of Accountancy Department, sent for Sani the day the school resumed classes. 'I suppose you know why I sent for you?' he said when Sani stepped into his office. His voice was very flat and cold. He noticed something that looked like the shape of a bottle in Sani's pocket. 'Sit up and take out what is in your pocket.'

Sani slowly brought out a little, green alcohol bottle. 'I'm sorry, Mallam!' He cried.

'You only feel sorry for yourself, you spoilt child.' Mallam got up and dusted off his long kaftan; he left the office and soon returned. 'Sani,' he said, 'believe it or not, no one is interested in drug slaves. Only fools engulf themselves in being a slave to drugs, like you have. I imagine how you must itch to get your hand on alcohol and a lot of drugs. Even when those that introduced you to Rohypnol, diazepam or cough syrups have been expelled, you never decide to change for a better life.

'You are not better than those who are gone; your performance is extremely low, and I'm afraid next semester is your last chance at this university. You'd better start thinking more about your future.'

'Yes, sir,' Sani said with a raspy voice.

'Leave my presence!' Mallam Suleiman said.

Later, Sani sat on the corner of his bunk, thinking, *How did I get myself into this drug slavery? It is every man's dream to have a certain future, but here I am, considered irresponsible.* He got up and began to wander around the room. *I was the fool who thought the idea up.*

It was fantastic at the start, but now it was rapidly developing into a nightmare. He went outside and sat under a tree, but then he got up and wandered to the open farmland which was opposite the hostel. *I will have to stop,* he concluded, thinking about Mallam Suleiman's words.

The following day, Sani stood in an unfinished room close to a deep hole. His hands were thrust deep into his trouser pockets, and his back was to the wall. He did not look up when a group of guys came in.

'He is alone now,' one of the guys said. Sani looked up and saw four young men he had fought with when his good friends were still at the school. 'He doesn't have to pretend to be the most powerful guy at this university anymore,' the young man said ponderously, dragging down a lungful of smoke.

'It's been a long time, hasn't it?' Sani wanted to avoid talking about what had happened.

'Listen,' the guy continued. 'You don't have to say anything about the fight. You and your boys beat up my friend fair and square. Nothing you could say would be new to me.'

The young man looked at him, and then he shifted his eyes. There was a long pause 'I'm sorry; I guess I wasn't thinking. Maybe I was on drugs that day,' Sani said.

'That is right; you weren't thinking,' the young man said and punched Sani's jaw. Sani, who was expecting that, shifted his head and countered with a heavy slap across the guy's face.

The blow stunned the guy, and he fell on his knees. The rest of the men walked over to Sani and started to hit him hard and poke his belly. The pain made tears run down his face, but he used his last bit of strength on them. He punched them, one after the other, very fast. The three young men knew that Sani was too strong and too smart for them; they ran out, leaving the first guy on the floor. The young man tried to hit Sani, but he protected himself with upraised arms.

Sani pushed the guy to the wall and went on slapping him. The young man fell to the ground. He hadn't the strength to resist him and was too dazed to speak. Sani put his hands into his attacker's pocket and brought out pinches of cocaine and a bottle of alcohol; the guy struggled and tried to snatch it away from him. 'You bitch, you are lucky I've not taken that back from you!' he said, but Sani was too quick for him. Sani shoved the guy away roughly, stood up, and put the drugs into his own pocket.

'Don't you dare come at me next time.' Sani knelt down beside him and smacked his face several times.

'Stop!' Two cadets came in, followed by the three other young men who had left earlier. 'We've had a lot of trouble from you.' They rushed Sani and searched of him, 'What is this? He is a drug slave.' they said as they took the drugs from his trouser pocket.

They tied Sani's hands tightly, pushed him out of the room and marched him down the path to the accountancy department.

The news soon reached Alhaji Umar. He walked to Mallam Suleiman's office, disappointed. After a talk, Alhaji Umar promised that he would play his fatherly role to help Sani change. He then ordered his driver to drive to a tall building, and he handed Sani over to the National Drug Law Enforcement Agency (NDLEA) for rehabilitation.

Chapter Six

Rehabilitation Centre

———⌒⌒———

William was living with his friend, Garba, in Isolo, a suburban part of the city and surviving on repairs of laptops, which he learned how to do from Garba. He always followed Garba to his shop and watched him troubleshoot many types of systems, and soon he also knew how to fix them.

Many police knew William as a troublemaker as a result of his behaviour fighting and stealing. Only those who were ignorant of him brought him their laptops to be fixed.

'William,' Garba said one day, 'When are you going to visit your father?'

'Isn't it a little soon? I just ran away from his house a couple of weeks ago.'

'That may be true, but it would be better if you go back and apologize,' Garba replied.

'Enough!' William shouted. 'You could have nicely told me to stop relying on your hospitality rather than pretending to be good.'

'No, you know I'd like you to stay, but . . . '

'But what? To hell with your advice,' William said finally, and he left hurriedly. He walked to a bar and bought himself a lot of drinks. *I think this will help an awful lot after hearing Garba's terrible advice,* he thought, looking at the long, crowded bar. He climbed onto a high stool carefully and sat down for a while after finishing his last drink.

As he left the bar, William walked on an express road. He passed a tall man standing very silently at the roadside, watching William until he turned onto an isolated path. The man's face was twisted with vicious fury. He jerked around and barked, 'Boys!' A good number of men moved hurriedly to obey.

William turned and saw some men in uniform following him. He made an effort to walk faster, and then he started running as he noticed the men running after him. The men finally caught up to him and grabbed him. William heard one of the men say, 'When you have good discipline at your advantage, you will learn that the best path in life is to stay away from drugs, not from your father's house.'

William stopped struggling against the men when he saw his father. He said, 'I know it's your doing, but this won't change me. It would be better if you ordered them to let go of me.' Mr Odibo instead ordered the men to tie William's hands behind his back.

William sat at the middle of the truck's back seat, and Mr Odibo was in the passenger seat as they drove to a big building that looked like a public dwelling. 'Do you like the way you are right now? Mr Odibo asked, looking at his son coldly. 'We will return home now if you promise to change,' he added.

'Why can't you stop these constant conversations that lead nowhere?' William shouted.

'He's starting trouble, and he needs to learn a good lesson. He's still acting tough.' One of the men interrupted.

'William, you raised a barrier which no family member, including me, could break through,' Mr Odibo said and sadly ordered the men to hand him over to the National Drug Law Enforcement Agency. 'Take him away!' ordered a tall man.

'William!' called Sani, who sat at the edge of a small bed in a big room at the NDLEA facility.

William was surprised. 'What happened that brought you here?' he asked

'Don't be silly. The end of every drug slave is sad, you know. I have changed, but I have to face the consequences of being a drug slave.'

'Wait a moment! Did I hear you say you changed?

'Yes, I had to change. I have lost the opportunity to be a university graduate, but I pray my father gives me another chance, and I will start over,' Sani said bitterly.

William laughed. 'Tell me about Buba, Ali, and Zubo.'

Sani shook his head. 'The school expelled them due to poor performance long before I graduated and went to the university.'

'How come you're here with me if you have truly changed?' William asked.

'It's a long story, but I will try to cut it short. I fought with some men at the university and collected pinches of cocaine and alcohol in their possession. Cadets caught us and searched me. They found the drugs on me, and then they handed me over to my father, who brought me here.'

An officer walked up and asked, 'Is one of you Sani?'

'Yes, sir,' Sani answered and followed the officer towards a man at a counter.

As he got closer, he was surprised to see his father. 'Daddy, I'm sorry!' he cried.

'I warned you several times, but you wouldn't listen,' Alhaji Umar said.

'I promise that I will never be a drug slave again. Please, Father, give me one last chance,' he pleaded. Alhaji Umar turned to a counsellor from the facility, and they discussed Sani's progress.

Minutes later, Sani begged his dad to let him say goodbye to his old friend. 'Be fast!' Alhaji Umar said as he agreed. 'William,' he called. 'Goodbye!' William watched, mouth agape, as Alhaji Umar and Sani walked out of the rehabilitation centre together.

About the Author

Ibrahim Muhammed Bashir is an Assistant State Commander of Operations and Intelligence with the National Drug Law Enforcement Agency (NDLEA) in Nigeria, West Africa. His experience in overseeing the activities of the Drug Demand Reduction Unit and his interactions with clients (known as Illicit Drug Abuse Persons) for a period of time has encouraged him to putting these stories into a book.

He is married with children. He golfs, plays badminton, and follows football keenly.

Synopsis

See the irony in the lives of Vincent, William, Sani, and their friends in school in this story of "drug slaves" in which children from humble family backgrounds are turned aside from responsible lives by negative influences and habits of different origins.

Experience the ordeal which misled the boys from their adolescence through their adulthood. They were transformed into miscreants and societal menaces, tormenting victims and traumatizing their families.

The drug which the children sought solace in due to family neglect, peer-group influence and other factors could only be better handled as they finally found themselves in a rehabilitation centre.